MAP MY HEART

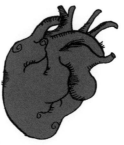

DOM & INK

sourcebooks

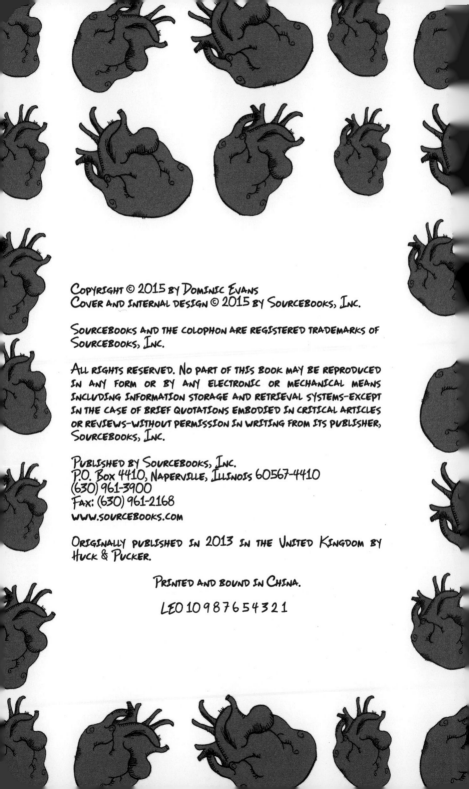

Published by Sourcebooks, Inc.
P.O. Box 4410, Naperville, Illinois 60567-4410
(630) 961-3900
Fax: (630) 961-2168
www.sourcebooks.com

Originally published in 2013 in the United Kingdom by
Huck & Pucker.

Printed and bound in China.

LEO 10 9 8 7 6 5 4 3 2 1

THIS
BOOK
BELONGS
TO

ABOUT THE AUTHOR

DOM&INK (ALSO KNOWN AS DOMINIC EVANS) IS AN ILLUSTRATOR AND DINOSAUR LOVER LIVING IN MANCHESTER. HE LOVES TRASHY TV, SKINNY JEANS, HAWAIIAN SHIRTS, AND COMICS. WHEN NOT TENDING TO HIS QUIFF, HE PRODUCES PATTERNS, EDITORIAL WORK, FASHION ILLUSTRATION, AND COMICS, AMONGST OTHER THINGS. HE LOVES A GOOD CUP OF TEA AND A BISCUIT TOO.

WWW. DOMANDINK.COM
@DOM_AND_INK

CONTENTS

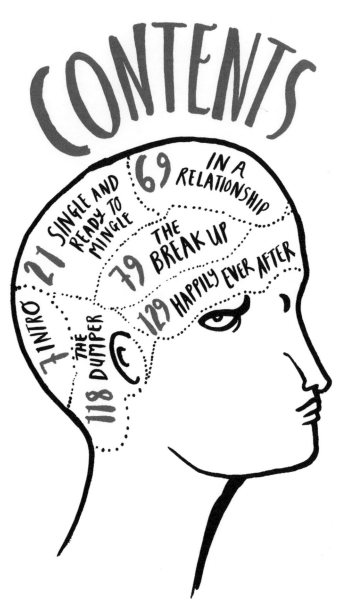

TURN THE PAGE TO START MAPPING THAT BIG OLD HEART OF YOURS →

INTRO

THIS BOOK, AT ONE POINT, WAS GOING TO BE CALLED "THE BIG BOOK OF RELATIONSHITS." THIS IS BECAUSE RELATIONSHITS CAN BE SHIT. PERSONALLY, I'M CRAP AT THEM, HOWEVER, I'M TOLD I'M GOOD AT GIVING ADVICE ON OTHER PEOPLE'S RELATIONSHITS. SO IF YOU'RE GETTING OVER TONY OR LEAVING RITA, OR MAYBE IF YOU FANCY TONY INSTEAD OF RITA, THIS BOOK IS FOR YOU. I HAVE ONE *RULE* FOR USING THIS BOOK: DO NOT BE FRAGILE. I WANT YOU TO SCRIBBLE, DEFACE, WRITE, DRAW, COLOR, AND RIP THIS BOOK WITHIN AN INCH OF ITS LIFE. CALL IT THERAPY.

SO STOP WEEPING INTO YOUR CARRYOUT, GRAB SOME FELT TIPS AND A BEER, AND GET READY FOR SOME **TOUGH LOVE.**

MY NOSE IS A LOT BIGGER THAN THIS IN 3D →

DRAW YOURSELF ON
THIS OLD POLAROID:

THIS IS ME

WHAT
IS
YOUR
RELATIONSHIP
STATUS?

(I RECOMMEND USING PENCIL HERE. TRUST ME.)

SO EMOTIONAL

TO REALLY GET SOMETHING FROM THIS BOOK, I NEED YOU
TO OPEN UP ABOUT YOUR EMOTIONS. SO STICK SOME POWER
BALLADS ON AND GET YOUR MARKERS OUT. IF YOU DON'T
LIKE THIS EXERCISE, TOUGH SHIT, YOU'RE DOING IT.
EXPRESS YOURSELF BY USING ANY SHAPE AND COLOR:

DRAW WHAT "HAPPY" LOOKS LIKE...

DRAW WHAT "I'M GONNA GET ME SOME LOVING TONIGHT" LOOKS LIKE...

DRAW WHAT "WHY HAVEN'T THEY TEXTED ME BACK YET" LOOKS LIKE...

DRAW WHAT "THE BEST KISS EVER" FEELS LIKE...

DRAW WHAT "I'M READY TO FIND LOVE AGAIN" LOOKS LIKE...

WOAH. THAT GOT INTENSE... NOW DRAW A CUTE PUPPY...

WHEREVER YOU ARE RIGHT NOW,
DRAW YOUR VIEW OUT OF YOUR
NEAREST WINDOW. I'VE LEFT IT
EMPTY SO YOU CAN ADD YOUR
OWN CURTAINS, PANES, AND LATCHES.
I KNOW, I'M REALLY NICE LIKE THAT.

THEN DRAW WHAT YOU *WANT* TO
SEE OUT OF YOUR OFFICE/BEDROOM/JAIL
CELL WINDOWS.

YOUR BRAIN FALLS IN LOVE IN THREE WAYS:

GETTIN' JIGGY

YOUR BRAIN IS DRIVEN BY ANDROGENS AND ESTROGENS. THESE GIVE YOU THE CRAVING FOR SEXUAL DESIRE. *FIFTY SHADES*, EAT YOUR HEART OUT. BOW CHIKKA WOH WOHHHH...

WHAT TURNS YOU ON?

TICK, CROSS, AND ADD YOUR OWN:

GINGERS ☐

HOT BODS ☐

EYE CONTACT ☐

SEXY ACCENTS ☐

FACIAL HAIR ☐

ATTACH

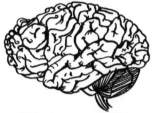

THAT SENSE OF CALM YOU FEEL IN A STABLE, LONG-TERM RELATIONSHIP IS FUELED BY THE HORMONES OXYTOCIN AND VASOPRESSIN. JUST LIKE LITTLE CUTE FLUFFY BUNNIES, THEY MAKE YOU FEEL ALL WARM AND FUZZY INSIDE. AWWWWW... DON'T GET USED TO IT.

USING ANY SHAPE AND COLOR, DRAW WARM AND FUZZY THINGS:

OBSESS

WHEN IN LOVE, YOUR DOPAMINE LEVELS INCREASE WHILE YOUR SEROTONIN DECREASES. THIS CAN CREATE MOOD SWINGS. ONE MINUTE YOU LOVE THEM, THE NEXT YOU HATE THEM. YOU WILL CRAVE THEM, OBSESS ABOUT THEM, AND FOCUS ALL YOUR THINKING ON THEM. BASICALLY, YOU'RE A PSYCHO. I BET MR. DARCY NEVER HAD THIS SHIT.

HOW DO YOU OBSESS? COMPLETE THE LIST:

FOLLOWING THEM
SMELLING CLOTHES
NON-STOP CALLING
NON-STOP TEXTING
"BUMPING" INTO THEM

TOUCH MY BODY

I WANT YOU TO GET IN TOUCH WITH THAT SEXY BODY OF YOURS. CONNECT THE BODY PART TO THE SAYING...

BRAIN	1. I'M MORE ATTRACTED TO A PRETTY ONE.
HEART	2. KISS IT.
FACE	3. I THINK I'M IN LOVE BUT... I'M NOT.
EYES	4. LET'S GET NAKED. NOW.
SEXUAL ORGANS	5. THEY ARE THE WINDOWS TO THE SOUL.
LEGS	6. I LOVE YOU.
ARSE	7. MINE IS WORTH A 1000 WORDS.
HANDS	8. I NEED THESE TO TEXT YOU TO PLAN A DATE.
SMILE	9. I USE THESE TO RUN AWAY FROM STALKERS AND... POLE DANCE.

THE TOP FIVE

WRITE THE FIVE BEST AND WORST THINGS
ABOUT YOU. NO PHYSICAL ATTRIBUTES ALLOWED.

PEOPLE LOVE ME BECAUSE:

1
2
3
4
5

I CAN BE A PAIN IN THE ARSE BECAUSE:

1
2
3
4
5

WE
ALL HAVE OUR
FAULTS.
INCLUDING YOU.
DEAL WITH IT.

WHERE DO YOU WANT TO BE IN FIVE YEARS' TIME?

FILL IN
THIS MYSTIC BALL
THAT LOOKS INTO THE FUTURE:

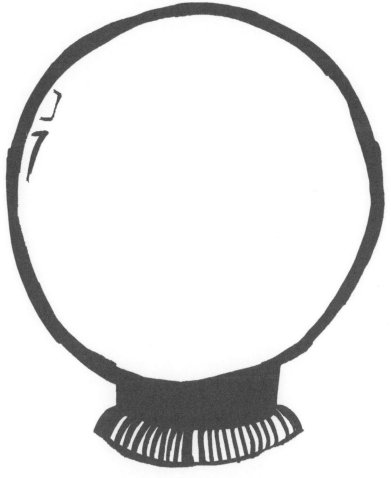

BEFORE THE NEXT CHAPTER ...

DO YOU WANT TO FIND LOVE?

YES ☐
NO ☐
PISS OFF ☐

IT'S TIME TO *REALLY* FIND OUT ⟶

SINGLE
&
READY TO
MINGLE

The
DEFINITES

WHEN LOOKING FOR LOVE, EVERYONE NEEDS "DEFINITES." THESE ARE KEY TRAITS IN FINDING A PERFECT PARTNER. FOR EXAMPLE, "MUST WANT KIDS/HAVE A GOOD JOB/BE CRAZY ABOUT CATS." IF SOMEONE DOESN'T FILL YOUR FOUR (MAYBE FIVE) DEFINITES, THEN KICK 'EM TO THE CURB!

WRITE YOURS DOWN HERE. NO PHYSICAL ATTRIBUTES ALLOWED!

CUT ME OUT AND KEEP ME IN A SAFE PLACE!

DRAW THE FIRST PERSON YOU EVER DATED:

DRAW THE PERSON YOU MOST RECENTLY DATED:

THE
OLD YOU

YOU NEED TO START DATING AGAIN BUT, LET'S FACE IT, YOU NEED A MAKEOVER. CUE A MONTAGE OF TRYING ON CLOTHES, DANCING TO '80s MUSIC, AND HIGH-FIVING FRIENDS. HELL YEAH!

CASE STUDY:

THIS IS WHAT I IMAGINE YOU LOOK LIKE AT THE MOMENT, EITHER MAUREEN, THE CRAZY CAT LADY WHO LIVES NEXT DOOR, OR PEDRO, THE NEW GUY AT WORK WHO SMELLS LIKE CABBAGES.

MAUREEN

PEDRO

WHAT DO YOU WANT TO FIX?

DRAW AND ADD WHAT YOU WANT TO FIX:

DRAW THE AWFUL, OLD
TURTLENECK SWEATER THAT
HAS KILLED YOUR SEX LIFE:

DRAW YOUR BUSHY EYEBROWS THAT
NEED PLUCKING:

DRAW AN ITEM OF CLOTHING YOU
OUGHT TO BURN!

MAKE A LIST OF NEW THINGS
TO BUY:
- a mirror
- soap
-
-
-
-
-
-
-
-
-

DRAW YOUR ROLE MODEL:

THE NEW YOU

WOW, YOU ARE LOOKING GOOD. I THINK I FANCY YOU A LITTLE NOW. WORK WITH WHAT YOU'VE GOT; YOU DON'T NEED A SIX-PACK OR LIPO TO BE ATTRACTIVE. IF YOU FEEL GREAT ON THE INSIDE, THEN YOU'LL LOOK GREAT ON THE OUTSIDE, BABY!

CASE STUDY:

MAUREEN AND PEDRO SCRUBBED UP WELL. QUITE LITERALLY. MAUREEN WASHED HER HAIR, PLUCKED HER EYEBROWS, AND DISCOVERED PUSH-UP BRAS. PEDRO HAD A SHOWER, THEN SEXED HIS HAIR UP WITH SOME WAX AND WORE A SWEATER HIS MUM DIDN'T KNIT HIM. GOOD WORK.

MAUREEN

COLOR THEM IN

PEDRO

WHAT **DID YOU FIX?**

NOW, DRAW WHAT YOU FIXED

DRAW YOUR NEWLY PLUCKED EYEBROWS:

↓   ↓

MAKE A LIST OF WHAT YOU DIDN'T CHANGE AND <u>WHY</u>:

1
2
3
4
5
6
7
8

DRAW THE NEW SEXY UNDERWEAR:

WHAT'S THE NAME OF YOUR NEW AFTERSHAVE/PERFUME?

USING SHAPES AND COLORS, DRAW YOUR NEWFOUND CONFIDENCE:

FILL THESE PAGES WITH THINGS YOU WANT IN YOUR PERFECT MATCH:

YOU'RE VERY HARD TO PLEASE, AREN'T YOU?

IMAGINE YOU'VE BEEN
SET UP ON A BLIND DATE.
AS YOU WALK UP TO THE
RESTAURANT, YOU CATCH
A GLIMPSE OF THEM
THROUGH THE WINDOW...
DRAW WHAT YOU WOULD
LIKE TO SEE.

WHAT TYPES OF *Dates* HAVE *YOU* HAD?

TICK THE BOXES OF THE TYPES OF DATES YOU'VE BEEN ON. BRINGING BACK SOME MEMORIES?

THE FACEBOOKER ☐

SO I MET YOU ON FACEBOOK. THEN YOU TWEETED ME AND LIKED MY STATUS UPDATE... WE WENT FOR A DRINK BUT THEN YOU DIDN'T LIKE MY NEW STATUS UPDATE?!

THE TEXTER ☐

SORRY I CAN'T MAKE IT TONIGHT. CAN WE RESCHEDULE? I KNOW IT'S THE FOURTH TIME I'VE STOOD YOU UP. IT'S JUST I'M REALLY SHY!

THE ANGRY DATER ☐

OUR DATE WENT REALLY WELL. BUT YOU'VE IGNORED ME SINCE... I'M SICK OF THIS SHIT! I NEVER WANT TO SEE YOU AGAIN, I HATE YOU! ARE YOU FREE ON TUESDAY TO HANG OUT?

THE SOCIAL CIRCLER ☐

SO LIKE, YEAH, WE MET AT THIS CLUB IN L.A. YOU SAID I WAS HOT AND THEN I REALIZED YOU'D SLEPT WITH MY FRIEND BUT THEN I REALIZED I'D SLEPT WITH ALL YOUR FRIENDS. YOU GETTING ME A DRINK OR WHAT?

THE BUNNY BOILER ☐

YOU NEVER REPLY TO MY TEXTS AND I'VE BEEN SITTING IN YOUR BUSHES FOR DAYS WAITING FOR YOU TO COME HOME... WE <u>WILL</u> BE TOGETHER! THINGS WILL BE BETTER WHEN WE'RE ALL BURIED IN THE GARDEN TOGETHER WITH MY PET RABBIT JERRY! I JUST WANT YOU TO LOVE ME, DEREK! LOVE ME!!

THE PRETTY ARSEHOLE ☐

I MODEL FOR A SMALL COMPANY CALLED BURBERRY, YOU HEARD OF IT? LOVE MY LIFE, LOVE MY JOB, LOVE MY FRIENDS. GOD, I'M BEAUTIFUL.

THE ONLINER ☐

I LOOK A BIT DIFFERENT IN 3D. THE PHOTO I SENT IS FROM 1996. NO, IT'S NOT ME EITHER. I HAVEN'T LEFT MY SHED FOR FIVE YEARS. THE INTERNET IS MY FRIEND.

YOU'RE STILL WAITING FOR THEM TO TEXT BACK.
IN THE MEANTIME, FINISH THIS PATTERN TO DISTRACT YOU...

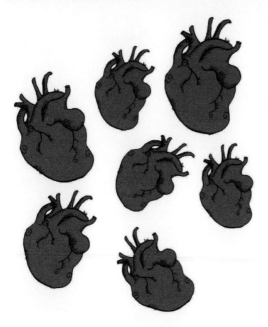

IT'S BEEN A WEEK SINCE THEY
LAST TEXTED YOU BACK. YOU'RE
GOING OUT TONIGHT AND HAVE
ALREADY DRUNK A BOTTLE
OF WINE. TO AVOID DRUNKENLY
SERENADING THEM ON THE
PHONE AT 2A.M., WRITE THEIR
NUMBER ON THIS NOTE AND HIDE
IT SOMEWHERE... OR MAYBE BURN IT?

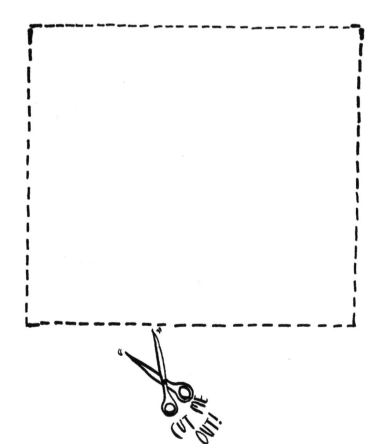

WE ARE EXCLUSIVE. JUST WHEN I DON'T SEE YOU I DATE OTHER PEOPLE.

ME ME ME

APPARENTLY YOU TALKED ABOUT YOURSELF TOO MUCH ON THE DATE. IT AIN'T ALL ABOUT YOU ... WRITE DOWN QUESTIONS TO ASK ON YOUR NEXT DATE. REMEMBER, IT'S ABOUT ENGAGING IN CONVERSATION, NOT INTERVIEWING THEM. NOW MEMORIZE YOUR QUESTIONS:

HOW TO SEDUCE

ON THE OPPOSITE PAGE IS A MASK. USING YOUR
EYES, STUDY THE MOUTH, THEN THE EYES, THEN
BACK TO THE MOUTH. REPEAT FIVE TIMES.
WELL DONE, YOU HAVE JUST "EYESEXED" SOMEONE.
THEY ARE NOW PUTTY IN YOUR HANDS.

NOW, DRAW THE REST OF THE FACIAL FEATURES.
I'VE INCLUDED BAD SKIN AND TEETH.
I NEVER SAID THEY WERE HOT. CUT OUT AND
USE AS A MASK OR STICK TO YOUR BEDROOM
 WALL AND START PRACTICING.

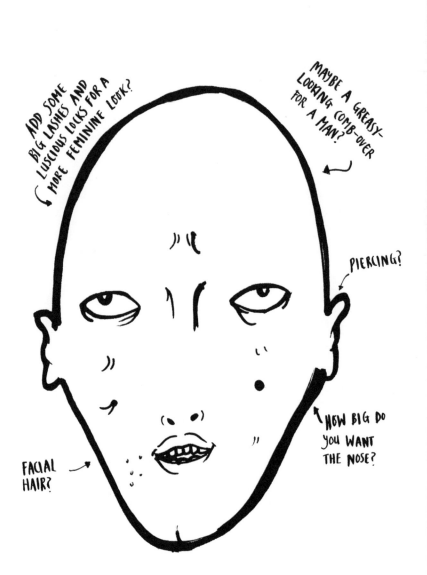

ADD SOME BIG LASHES AND LUSCIOUS LOCKS FOR A MORE FEMININE LOOK?

MAYBE A GREASY-LOOKING COMB-OVER FOR A MAN?

PIERCING?

FACIAL HAIR?

HOW BIG DO YOU WANT THE NOSE?

EYESEX ALL THESE PEOPLE...
THEN GIVE THEM NAMES!

THE DODGY PORN STAR

THE FASHIONISTA

THE GIRL AT WORK WHO IS
ALWAYS MOANING

THE MODEL/ACTOR/DANCER

THE GUY FROM NEXT DOOR
WHO HAS B.O.

THE BUNNY BOILER

THE REALLY BORING FRIEND

THE PLASTIC-SURGERY-ADDICTED COUGAR

41

WRITE YOUR PERFECT
Date...

THEIR NAME:

THEIR JOB:

THE BAR YOU GO TO FOR THE FIRST TEN AWKWARD MINUTES:

THEIR FAVORITE MUSIC:

NUMBER OF TIMES THEY EYESEX YOU:

WHO IS YOUR MUTUAL FACEBOOK FRIEND?:

THE DRINK YOU ORDER:

WHAT THEY ARE WEARING:

NOW WRITE HOW THE *Date* REALLY WENT...

THEIR CHEAP EAU DE TOILETTE:

YOUR CHEAP EAU DE TOILETTE:

THE TIME YOU REALIZE YOU DON'T FANCY THEM:

DO YOU WANT THEM TO TEXT YOU AFTER?

DO YOU EVEN FANCY THEM?

DO YOU REALLY GIVE A SHIT?

NOW GIVE YOUR SCORE.  /10

CHOIR PRACTICE

"SO IT'S BEEN THREE DATES AND THEY WENT REALLY WELL. THEN HE JUST STOPPED SPEAKING TO ME. I THEN LEFT A VOICE MAIL BUT HE TEXTED ME WEEKS LATER AND SAID 'I'M REALLY SORRY, I'VE BEEN ILL AND BEEN BUSY WITH CHOIR PRACTICE, AND MY EX HAS GOTTEN BACK IN TOUCH AND FUCKED WITH MY HEAD. SORRY'.
THAT'S THE LAST I HEARD FROM HIM, I FEEL LIKE SHIT."

DATE FROM HELL

WRITE DOWN YOUR WORST DATE. LIKE EVER.

WHO?

WHEN?

WHERE?

DID THEY SMELL
LIKE CHEESE?

THE CREEPIEST
MOMENT:

45

DRAW ALL THE FACES OF THE PEOPLE YOU HAVE EVER BEEN ON DATES WITH:

THAT MANY, EH?

47

WILLIAM SHAKESPEARE

(APRIL 26, 1564 — APRIL 23, 1616)

SHAKESPEARE WAS AN ENGLISH
PLAYWRIGHT AND POET. MANY OF
HIS PLAYS DEALT WITH RELATIONSHIPS
AND HUMAN NATURE, AMONGST
OTHER THINGS. I LIKE TO THINK
IF HE WERE AROUND TODAY
WE WOULD BE BEST MATES.

THE *JIGGY* CHAIN

NOWADAYS, YOU CAN'T DATE A NICE PERSON WITHOUT FINDING THEY'VE SLEPT WITH/SEXTED/DATED/DUMPED OR BEEN STAMP COLLECTING WITH SOMEONE YOU KNOW. MAKE YOUR OWN JIGGY CHAIN BY DRAWING YOUR FRIENDS AND THEN CONNECTING THEM TO WHO THEY DID THE DIRTY WITH:

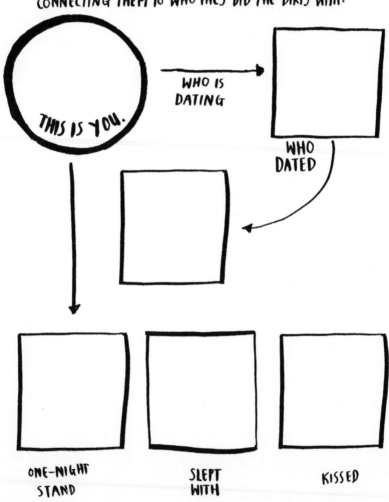

THIS IS YOU.

WHO IS DATING

WHO DATED

ONE-NIGHT STAND

SLEPT WITH

KISSED

50

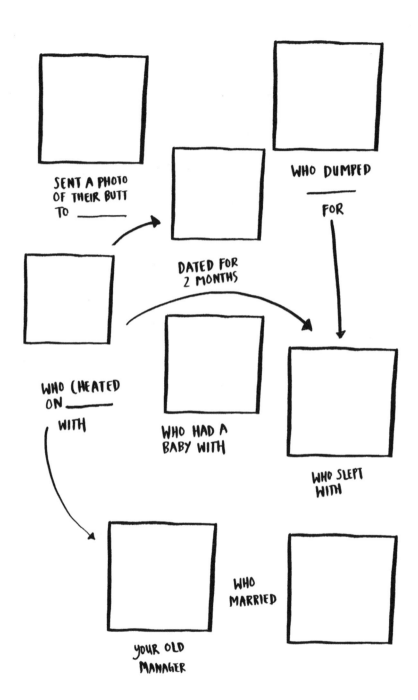

SENT A PHOTO
OF THEIR BUTT
TO _____

WHO DUMPED
_____
FOR

DATED FOR
2 MONTHS

WHO CHEATED
ON _____
WITH

WHO HAD A
BABY WITH

WHO SLEPT
WITH

WHO
MARRIED

YOUR OLD
MANAGER

51

WRITE A LIST OF WHAT YOU WANT IN YOUR NEXT PARTNER

TEAR HERE

- THEY HAVE TO BE ABSOLUTELY BEAUTIFUL
- LOADSA MONEY. MILLIONAIRE IF POSSIBLE
- OWNS A HELICOPTER AND "HOUSE STAFF"
- MUST LIKE CATS

— UNLIMITED PAPER

NOW, WRITE A LIST OF WHAT YOU WANT
IN YOUR NEXT PARTNER (BE REALISTIC)

(ON THIS VERY SMALL PIECE OF PAPER)

THE PUPIL OF YOUR
EYE CAN EXPAND AS
MUCH AS 45% WHEN
LOOKING AT SOMEONE
YOU LOVE.

DRAW YOUR PUPILS WHEN...

A. YOU SEE DEREK, THAT ONE-NIGHT STAND YOU HAD THREE MONTHS AGO. HE HAD A REALLY HAIRY BACK.

B. YOU'RE AT THE SUPERMARKET CHECKOUT AND THE PERSON YOU'VE BEEN SPEAKING TO ON FACEBOOK (YOU'VE NEVER MET) IS SELLING YOU A SPANISH SAUSAGE.

C. YOU SEE MAUREEN THE CAT LADY FROM DOWNSTAIRS. DAMN SHE'S LOOKING GOOD.

D. YOU SEE THE LOVE OF YOUR LIFE.

IF SOMEONE CAN HOLD
EYE CONTACT WITH YOU
FOR FIVE SECONDS, IT
MEANS THEY'RE ATTRACTED
TO YOU. NOW TURN AROUND,
OPEN YOUR EYES, AND
FLIRT!

STAND A PEN IN THE MIDDLE OF THE CLOCK. DROP IT, LIKE IT'S HOT, THEN WHATEVER O'CLOCK IT LANDS ON, YOU HAVE TO SPIN AROUND, FIND THE NEAREST PERSON IN THAT DIRECTION, AND FLIRT.

YOU'RE AT THE
MOVIE THEATER
ON A DATE. DRAW THE
FILM YOU'RE WATCHING...

PUMP UP THE VOLUME

SCIENTISTS SAY THAT A GOOD TUNE CAN INCREASE SEROTONIN LEVELS, WHICH THEN CREATE POSITIVE EFFECTS ON A NUMBER OF THINGS INCLUDING MOOD, MEMORY POWER, AND SEXUAL DESIRE. MAKE A PRE-DATE PLAYLIST TO BOOST THOSE SEROTONIN LEVELS THROUGH THE ROOF.

♫♫ TRACKLIST ♫♫

1
2
3
4
5
6
7
8
9
10
11
12

DESIGN YOUR OWN CD COVER:

DRAW YOUR
BEST DATE OUTFIT
KNOCK 'EM DEAD!

NOW
DESIGN YOUR OWN
SEXY UNDERWEAR

ADD SOME PATTERNS TO THESE SEDUCTIVE PIECES!

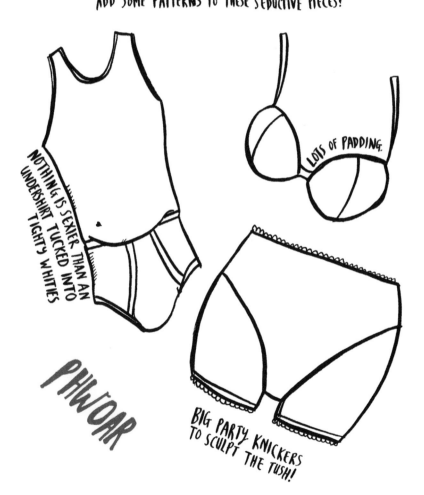

NOTHING IS SEXIER THAN AN UNDERSHIRT TUCKED INTO TIGHTY WHITIES

LOTS OF PADDING.

PHWOAR

BIG PARTY KNICKERS TO SCULPT THE TUSH!

YOU'RE GOING TO NEED A LOT MORE COCKTAILS BEFORE YOU FIND YOUR DATE MORE ATTRACTIVE... DRAW THEIR REFLECTION THROUGH THE GLASS AND HOW MUCH BETTER THEY LOOK AFTER YOUR SIXTH MARTINI.

BEFORE

AFTER

WHEN PEOPLE HEAR WHAT THEY WANT TO HEAR

THE THING IS, I THINK YOU'RE SUCH A GOOD PERSON. YOU MAKE ME LAUGH SO MUCH! IT'S JUST THAT I'M REALLY CONFUSED AS TO WHAT I WANT, AND I KNOW IT WILL NEVER BE YOU. I'M NOT SEXUALLY OR EMOTIONALLY ATTRACTED TO YOU AT ALL. IN FACT, PLEASE STOP TEXTING AND CALLING ME. SERIOUSLY, IT IS NEVER GONNA HAPPEN!

FILL IN THE BLANKS OF WHAT YOU WANT TO HEAR:

AWWWWWWW! THEY SAID I'M A........... PERSON, AND THAT I MAKE THEM............! THEY'RE SO SWEET TO ME.

FACE 2 FACE

SO MY FRIEND WAS ON A DATE HAVING DINNER WITH A GUY WHEN HIS PHONE RECEIVED A TEXT FROM HIS DATE. PUZZLED, MY FRIEND READ THE TEXT: "OMG THIS DATE IS SO BORING AND HE HAS A HUGE FOREHEAD. I CAN'T WAIT TO GO HOME." THERE WAS A LONG SILENCE AS THE DATE REALIZED THEY HAD TEXTED THE WRONG PERSON. MY FRIEND WENT,

"LET'S GET THE BILL."

IN ONE WORD, HOW
ARE YOU FEELING RIGHT
NOW?

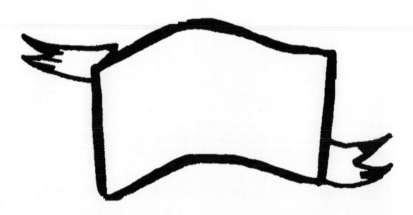

IN
A
RELATIONSHIP

WRITE DOWN ALL THE THINGS YOU LIKE IN YOUR NEW PARTNER

▶ THEY LISTEN TO ME

▶ THEY LAUGH AT <u>ALL</u> MY JOKES

▶ THEY DON'T CARE WHAT CRAP I EAT

▶

▶

▶

▶

▶

▶

▶

▶

▶

▶

▶

▶

▶

▶

▶

YOUR FRIENDS

WHAT DO THEY THINK OF YOUR NEW PARTNER? STEAL THEIR PASSPORT PHOTOS, STICK 'EM IN, AND WRITE WHAT THEY THINK:

THE BEST FRIEND SAYS:

THE GOBBY, LOUD, RUDE FRIEND SAYS:

THE BITCHY FRIEND SAYS:

THE FRIEND WHO IS ALWAYS THERE FOR YOU AND IS SECRETLY IN LOVE WITH YOU SAYS:

THE FRIEND YOU ACTUALLY DON'T KNOW WHY YOU'RE FRIENDS WITH SAYS:

WHAT DOES YOUR MOM THINK OF YOUR NEW LOVER?

ASK YOUR MOM TO FILL THIS BOX IN
WITH HER "OPINIONS".

(FACE IT. SHE HATES THEM.)

WHEN WE'RE TOGETHER I PUT ON AN ACT. THE REAL ME IS ACTUALLY A DICK. YOU'LL FIND OUT SOON ENOUGH.

DRAW SOME OF THE BEST THINGS YOU AND YOUR PARTNER HAVE DONE TOGETHER:

HOW
THEY RUINED
THE
RELATIONSHIP

MAKE A SHORT LIST:

1 THEY CHECKED YOUR PHONE
2 THEY CALLED YOU FAT
3 THEY TOOK YOUR MONEY
4 THEY SLEPT WITH YOUR BEST FRIEND
5 THEY'RE ALWAYS LATE
6 THEY CALLED YOU FAT AGAIN
7
8
9
10
11
12

(CONTINUE ON A SEPARATE SHEET IF YOU NEED TO)

HOW DID *YOU* RUIN THE RELATIONSHIP?

MAKE A SHORT LIST:

1 I KISSED THEIR BEST FRIEND
2 I READ THEIR DIARY AND TOLD ALL MY FRIENDS
3 I USED THEIR CREDIT CARD... MAYBE TWICE... OK, FOUR TIMES
4 I BOILED THEIR PET BUNNY CALLED BARNEY
5
6
7
8
9
10
11
12

ON AVERAGE, MOST RELATIONSHIPS
LAST 3 TO 5 MONTHS. I'D KEEP
THE RECEIPT FOR THAT TRIP
YOU JUST BOOKED, THEN.

HOW LONG DID YOURS LAST?

YEARS	MONTHS	DAYS

HOURS	MINUTES	SECONDS

THE

BREAK

UP

THIS IS THE MOMENT YOU CAME HOME EARLY AND SAW YOUR PARTNER CHEATING ON YOU THROUGH THE KEYHOLE. DRAW WHAT YOU SAW, THEN RIP IT UP.

NOTHING COMPARES 2U

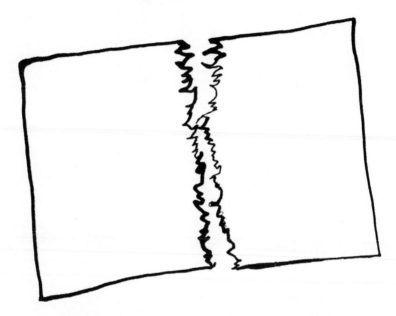

YOU'VE HAD SINÉAD O'CONNOR ON ALL NIGHT.
YOU'RE DRUNK AND HAVE WORK AT 8AM.
DRAW YOU AND YOUR EX IN HAPPIER TIMES,
THEN DEFACE THE SHREDDED PHOTO WITH
OBSCENE LANGUAGE THAT WOULD SHOCK
YOUR MOTHER.

I DON'T LOVE YOU. ANYMORE. IT'S OVER. BUT I WILL CONTINUE TO SLEEP WITH YOU AND MESS WITH YOUR HEAD.

THERE ARE 2 STAGES OF REJECTION...

PROTEST

DESIGN YOUR OWN BOX OF CHOCOLATES TO WIN YOUR EX BACK WITH:

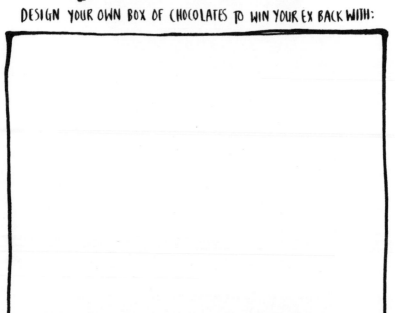

YOU'VE JUST BROKEN UP BUT YOU'RE DETERMINED
TO WIN YOUR EX BACK. HOWEVER, YOU MAY TURN INTO
A BUNNY BOILER TRYING TO DISSECT WHERE YOU WENT
WRONG. THIS IS THEN FOLLOWED BY YOU STALKING THEM
AT THEIR WORK, FAVORITE BAR, OR EVEN THEIR HOUSE.
THEY DON'T ANSWER YOUR SOBBING CALLS, FACEBOOK
POKES, OR LONG TEXTS. WHEN IN DOUBT, BOIL THEIR
BUNNY. OR DOG. OR BRIDGE.

FOLLOWED BY THE LOVELY STAGE OF...

DESPAIR

DRAW WHAT YOUR FACE LOOKS LIKE WHEN YOU CRY:

THIS IS THE BIT WHEN YOU FEEL REALLY CRAPPY.
YOU'LL CRY, MOAN, WHINE, STARE INTO SPACE,
GET DRUNK, SKIP WORK, THROW UP, AND CRY
SOME MORE. YOUR BRAIN IS ON OVERLOAD AND
STARTS TO SPUTTER OUT INCREASED DOPAMINE
LEVELS, WHICH CAN CAUSE LETHARGY AND DEPRESSION.
EVERYTHING IS SHIT. LIFE IS SHIT. WORK IS SHIT.
BLAH BLAH BLAH BLAH BLAH.

LET'S HAVE A PITY PARTY!

YOU SPEND MOST EVENINGS SOBBING INTO LAST NIGHT'S CARRYOUT WHILE TEXTING ALL YOUR FRIENDS, REMINDING THEM HOW SHITTY YOU FEEL. THIS IS A PERFECT TIME FOR A PITY PARTY. THESE ARE YOUR BARE ESSENTIALS...

1: TRASH TV

DRAW WHAT YOU'RE WATCHING TONIGHT:

VHS

TRASH TV IS CRUCIAL IN YOUR PERIOD OF SELF-DESPAIR. ANY REALITY SHOW IS PERFECT PITY-PARTY FODDER. IT IS ACTUALLY PROVEN THAT YOUR SELF-CONFIDENCE IN LOOKS AND LIFE GOALS WILL INCREASE BY AT LEAST 100% BY WATCHING ANY TALK SHOW. BRING ON THE TRASH.

2: CARRYOUT

YOU HAVEN'T EATEN FOR DAYS AND CAN'T BE
BOTHERED TO BUY GROCERIES. SPEND AN INSANE
AMOUNT OF MONEY ON AN INSANE AMOUNT OF
FOOD THAT YOU WILL NEVER FINISH EATING.
ADD A TOPPING TO YOUR PIZZA, THEN COLOR
IN *THE PIZZA PIE CHART* TO SHOW HOW
SHITTY YOU FEEL TONIGHT:

3: ICE CREAM

IT HAS TO COME FROM A HUGE TUB, NOT A LITTLE MINI ONE, HELL NO. A HUGE, INSANELY EXPENSIVE TUB. MAYBE TWO. WHAT FLAVOR DID YOU BUY? DESIGN A TUB AND GIVE IT A DELICIOUS NAME:

4: SITTING ON YO' FAT ASS

AN ELASTIC WAISTBAND IS THE WAY FORWARD. YOU WILL NEED SOME PANTS WITH ONE, AS HOW ELSE WILL YOU FIT ALL THAT FOOD IN? REMEMBER, DON'T WASH THEM. IF YOU WANT TO TRULY FESTER THEY NEED TO GET DIRTY. DRAW SOME PIZZA AND GREASE STAINS ON YOUR STRETCHY PANTS.

5: GET THE MESSAGE

MAKE SURE YOU TEXT ALL YOUR FRIENDS TELLING THEM HOW SHITTY YOU FEEL. THEY ALL REALLY WANT TO KNOW. NO, REALLY, THEY DO. KEEP CHECKING YOUR PHONE... IF YOU STAY AS PARANOID AS POSSIBLE AND CHECK YOUR PHONE EVERY 3 MINUTES, IT IS PROVEN TO IMPROVE REFLEXES AND HAND-TO-EYE COORDINATION.

NO ONE HAS TEXTED YOU LOL

WRITE DOWN ALL THE TEXTS YOU HAVE SENT/RECEIVED TONIGHT

6: MAKE A PITY PLAYLIST

IF YOU'RE GOING TO WALLOW IN SELF-PITY, YOU MAY AS WELL DO IT IN STYLE. MAKE A MIX CD TO SOB INTO YOUR PIZZA TO. YOU ARE ALLOWED <u>ONE</u> ADELE OR COLDPLAY SONG. JUST ONE!

DESIGN YOUR OWN CD COVER

TRACKLIST

1
2
3
4
5
6
7
8
9
10

7: SOCIAL STALKER

YOU'VE BEEN STALKING YOUR EX ON FACEBOOK AND TWITTER, CONSTANTLY REFRESHING THE PAGE BECAUSE YOU'VE REALIZED THAT NO ONE (LITERALLY NO ONE) HAS COMMENTED ON YOUR STATUS UPDATE. TOTES DRAMA. NOW WRITE ALL THE MELODRAMATIC TWEETS AND STATUS UPDATES YOU HAVE SHARED. READ THEM BACK OVER TOMORROW. YES, YOU SHOULD BE EMBARRASSED.

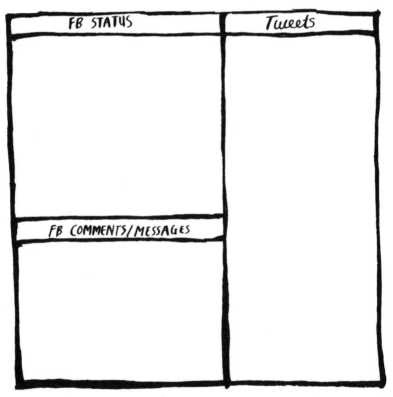

FB STATUS	Tweets

FB COMMENTS/MESSAGES

DELETE FACEBOOK: OR TWITTER, OR TUMBLR, OR ALL OF 'EM. WHETHER SHORT-TERM OR LONG-TERM, IT RESULTS IN AVOIDING AWFUL PHOTO TAGS, LIKES, AND DRUNKEN STATUS UPDATES. ALSO, IT'S INTERESTING TO SEE HOW MANY PEOPLE NOTICE YOU'VE GONE. TREAT IT LIKE A SOCIAL EXPERIMENT.

DESCRIBE YOUR EX IN AS MANY SWEAR WORDS AS POSSIBLE:

DOES YOUR MOTHER KNOW YOU HAVE A MOUTH LIKE A SEWER?!

TEAR

RIP

THE ANGRY PAGE!

ALL THAT SWEARING
HAS PROBABLY LEFT
YOU FEELING PRETTY
PISSED OFF. RIP THIS
PAGE OUT IN ANGER
AND SCREAM AS YOU
TEAR IT TO SHREDS.
DO YOU FEEL BETTER?

RIP

TEAR

YOU KNOW IT'S GOING TO HAPPEN AT THE WORST TIME. IT ALWAYS DOES. BUMPING INTO YOUR EX FOR THE FIRST TIME SINCE SPLITTING IS ALWAYS SHIT. WRITE WHAT YOU WOULD SAY IN THE SPEECH BUBBLE:

REPEAT THIS IN THE MIRROR TEN TIMES A DAY.

ARTHUR SCHOPENHAUER
(FEBRUARY 22, 1788 - SEPTEMBER 21, 1860)

ARTHUR WAS A GERMAN PHILOSOPHER.
HIS THEORY WAS THAT RELATIONSHIPS ARE
THE MAIN SOURCE OF STRESS AND HURT.
HIS WORK HAS BEEN REGARDED AS
PESSIMISTIC. DESPITE THAT, HE'S WRITTEN
SOME CRACKING ONE-LINERS.

WHAT WE'RE ATTRACTED TO IS NOT ALWAYS BEST FOR US.

THE REJECTION SURVIVAL KIT

NOW THE PITY PARTY HAS COME AND GONE, YOU NEED TO EMBRACE THE MOMENT. I'M NOT SAYING CHANGE YOUR WHOLE LIFE, HOWEVER, THERE ARE SMALL SOLUTIONS THAT CAN GET YOU THROUGH THE BIG BLACK HOLE OF *REJECTION*.

THE *NEW* DO!

A NEW HAIRCUT WILL ALWAYS MAKE YOU FEEL BETTER. HAIR IS YOUR BEST ACCESSORY, SO IF YOU GET THIS RIGHT, YOUR CONFIDENCE WILL BE SKY-HIGH. A DRASTIC CHANGE IN APPEARANCE ALSO REFLECTS THE CHANGES GOING ON WITHIN. STICK PHOTOS OF BEFORE AND AFTER BELOW:

THE *OLD* DO!   THE *NEW* DO!

The CARD OF *DOOM*

I'M NOT SAYING GET INTO DEBT BY ANY MEANS. OKAY, ACTUALLY I KIND OF AM. A LITTLE TREAT IS NECESSARY NOW AND THEN...
HOW ELSE ARE YOU GOING TO AFFORD THE NEW HAIRCUT OR THAT NEW SHIRT ON EBAY? FORGET IT! JUST THIS ONCE...

I WANT TO SEE A PHOTO OF YOU MODELING YOUR LATEST PURCHASE:

WORK IT, BABY

YOUR FRIENDS ARE *SICK* OF YOU

YOUR FRIENDS HAVE BEEN AMAZING. THEY'VE STOOD BY YOU, FED YOU CHOCOLATE, AND ANSWERED YOUR 11 P.M. DRUNKEN, SOBBING PHONE CALLS (YES - YOU DID GET THAT DRUNK. SEE BELOW). HOWEVER, THERE WILL COME A TIME WHEN YOUR FRIENDS WILL BE BORED OF YOU GOING ON ABOUT YOUR EX.

EVERYBODY IN THE CLUB GETTIN' TIPSAY:

NOW, ALCOHOL SHOULD NOT ALWAYS BE THE FIRST THING TO RELY ON. IT SHOULD BE THE SECOND. WHILE IT WILL HELP YOU LOSE YOUR INHIBITIONS, THAT ISN'T ALWAYS A GOOD THING. DRINK RESPONSIBLY AND YOU WON'T BECOME THE HOT MESS THAT GETS NAKED, THROWS UP, CALLS PEOPLE, OR ATTEMPTS KARAOKE BEFORE 9 P.M.

YOUR FAMILY

DRAW YOUR FAMILY HERE:

IN TIMES OF NEED, SUPPORT COMES FROM EVERYWHERE. YOUR MOM IS ALWAYS A GREAT PERSON FOR HUGS AND ADVICE. IF NOT YOUR MOM, THEN MAYBE YOUR DAD, COUSIN, SISTER, OR JOLLY UNCLE. EITHER WAY, FAMILY IS ALWAYS THERE FOR YOU. ALSO, YOU KNOW YOU'LL GET A DECENT BREW AND COOKIE AFTER.

FANCY A HUG?

WINSTON CHURCHILL
(NOVEMBER 30, 1874 - JANUARY 24, 1965)

CHURCHILL WAS THE PRIME MINISTER OF THE UNITED KINGDOM FROM 1940 TO 1945 (AGAIN FROM 1951 TO 1955). HE WAS SEEN AS A GREAT WARTIME LEADER AND ALSO THE ONLY BRITISH PRIME MINISTER IN HISTORY TO HAVE RECEIVED THE NOBEL PRIZE FOR LITERATURE.

IF YOU'RE GOING THROUGH HELL, KEEP GOING.

HEAD vs. HEART

THERE ARE TWO TYPES OF PEOPLE; THOSE WHO THINK
AND THOSE WHO FEEL. WHAT DO YOU USE MORE?

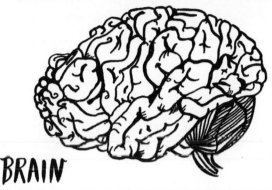

BRAIN

IF YOU USE YOUR BRAIN, YOU ARE MORE LIKELY TO
THINK METHODICALLY ABOUT A RELATIONSHIP RATHER
THAN YOUR FEELINGS TOWARD SOMEONE. FACTS COME
FIRST, EMOTIONS SECOND. BASICALLY, YOU ARE A
ROBOT... OR AN ARSEHOLE.

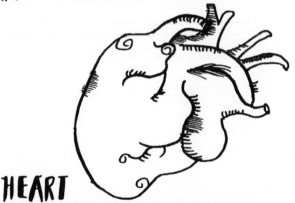

HEART

IF YOU USE YOUR HEART, YOU ARE MORE LIKELY
TO TAKE THE BIGGER PICTURE INTO ACCOUNT,
HOWEVER, YOUR FEELINGS WILL ALWAYS WIN
OVER FACTS. ALSO, YOU ARE MORE LIKELY TO
BE CONSTANTLY HURT BY RELATIONSHIPS AS YOU
ARE MORE WILLING TO TAKE A RISK FOR THE
SAKE OF LOVE.

YOUR EX WANTS TO GET BACK TOGETHER... WEIGH THE OPTIONS BY LISTING REASONS WHY YOU _THINK_ YOU SHOULD AND WHY YOU _FEEL_ YOU SHOULD...

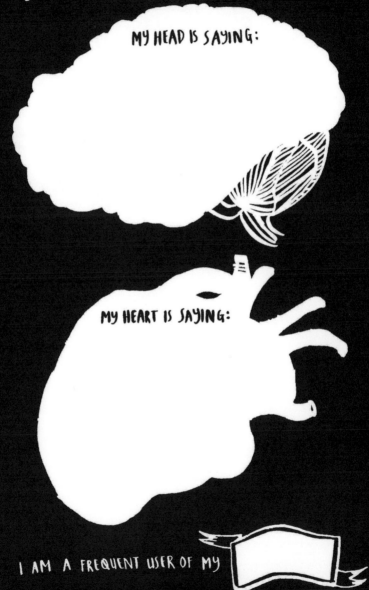

MY HEAD IS SAYING:

MY HEART IS SAYING:

I AM A FREQUENT USER OF MY

COLOR ME IN...

SOME

ARE MEANT

LOVE

BE.

PEOPLE TO FALL IN BUT NOT TOGETHER

THE
GOOD TIMES

THE MAIN ADVANTAGE OF BEING
RECENTLY SINGLE IS THAT YOU
GET WAY MORE CRAP DONE DAILY.
YOUR FAMILY AND FRIENDS HAVE
JOINED YOU ON DAYS OUT, DINNERS,
PARTIES, AND PROBABLY SOME BINGO.
STICK PHOTOS IN AND COVER THE
PATTERN ON THE NEXT PAGE WITH
RECENT MEMORABLE MOMENTS.
THEN CUT IT OUT AND FRAME IT.

THE COMEBACK

JUST LIKE MADONNA DOES EVERY TWO YEARS, YOU'RE MAKING A COMEBACK, BABY. YOU'VE GOT THE NEW 'DO, GOT FIT, AND GOT A NEW STYLE. IMAGINE THE MOMENT YOU WALK INTO A BAR, YOU STOP AT THE DOOR, EVERYBODY TURNS TO SEE YOU AS THE MUSIC BUILDS TO A CRESCENDO... DRAW THAT MOMENT... NOW!

COLOR THIS IN...
TRY
NOT TO LOSE
FAITH AND MORALS
AFTER ONE BAD
EXPERIENCE

NOW YOU'RE FEELING BETTER AND GETTING YOUR SWAGGER BACK. THERE ARE STILL BAD DAYS, BUT WE ALL GET THEM. STICK A PHOTO IN TO SHOW HOW GOOD YOU'RE LOOKING NOW.

Oh baby, you looking so DAMN FINE!

FILL THESE BOXES WITH SIX SHORT-TERM GOALS YOU WANT TO ACHIEVE IN THE NEXT SIX WEEKS:

IT'S THE FIRST TIME YOU
HAVE SEEN YOUR EX IN
A YEAR... THEY'RE STANDING
AT THE BAR AND HAVEN'T
NOTICED YOU YET. DRAW
THEM BEHIND THIS CROWD
OF DRUNKEN PEOPLE...

GET THIS TATTOOED ON YOUR BOTTOM

REJECTION IS GOD'S PROTECTION

Everything Happens For A Reason..

NOW DESIGN YOUR OWN TATTOOS
FOR SOMEONE ELSE'S BOTTOM:

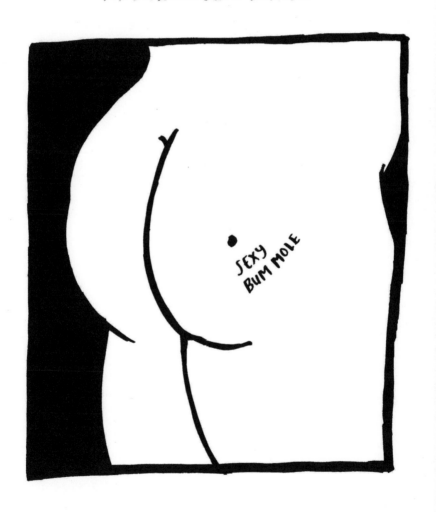

MAYBE YOU'RE THE ONE DOING THE DUMPING.
FACE IT, YOU'VE BEEN SICK OF YOUR PARTNER
FOR WEEKS. YOU'VE REALIZED THEY'RE SELFISH,
STUPID, AND STINGY. THAT'S A TRIPLE THREAT.
WRITE YOUR FINAL WORDS ON THIS POST-IT
YOU HAVE LEFT FOR THEM TO FIND:

CUT ME
OUT!

IF THIS FAILS, TRY THESE METHODS.
TICK WHEN COMPLETED:

I BROKE UP BY ...   FACEBOOK ☐

CARRIER
PIGEON ☐

TELLING
THEIR MOM ☐

119

DRAW WHAT YOUR RELATIONSHIP WAS LIKE WHEN YOU FIRST GOT TOGETHER:

NOW DRAW WHAT IT WAS LIKE AT THE END:

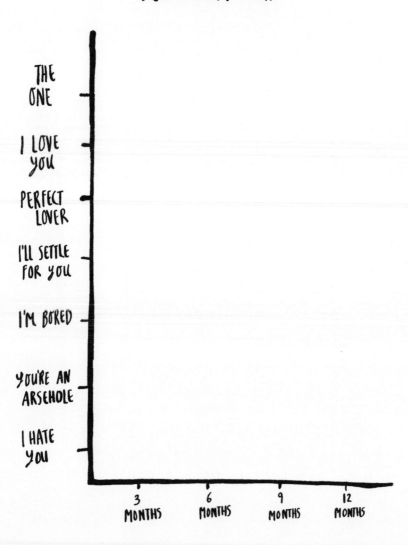

LET'S MAKE A LINE GRAPH OF YOUR
RELATIONSHIP

THE
ONE

I LOVE
YOU

PERFECT
LOVER

I'LL SETTLE
FOR YOU

I'M BORED

YOU'RE AN
ARSEHOLE

I HATE
YOU

3
MONTHS

6
MONTHS

9
MONTHS

12
MONTHS

GET THIS PRINTED ONTO A T-SHIRT

KICK 'EM TO THE CURB!

WHAT DID THEY PUT INTO THE RELATIONSHIP?

WHAT DID YOU PUT INTO THE RELATIONSHIP?

MICHELLE OBAMA

(JANUARY 17, 1964 - PRESENT)

MICHELLE IS THE WIFE OF THE 44TH
PRESIDENT OF THE UNITED STATES,
BARACK OBAMA. ASIDE FROM BEING THE
FIRST AFRICAN AMERICAN FIRST LADY,

SHE IS A WRITER AND USED TO BE A
LAWYER. I DON'T THINK SHE COULD GET
ANY MORE AMAZING.

DO NOT

BRING PEOPLE IN YOUR LIFE WHO WEIGH YOU DOWN. AND TRUST YOUR INSTINCTS... GOOD RELATIONSHIPS FEEL GOOD. THEY FEEL RIGHT. THEY DON'T HURT. THEY'RE NOT PAINFUL. THAT'S NOT JUST WITH SOMEBODY YOU WANT TO MARRY, BUT IT'S WITH THE FRIENDS THAT YOU CHOOSE. IT'S WITH THE PEOPLE YOU SURROUND YOURSELVES

WITH.

127

WHY ARE YOU LEAVING THEM?

ANSWER IN JUST THREE WORDS...

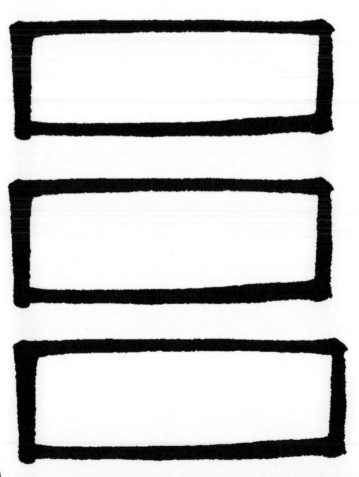

YOU'RE FEELING EMPOWERED. USING SHAPES AND COLORS, DRAW YOUR NEWFOUND CONFIDENCE. LET'S GET ABSTRACT, BABY.

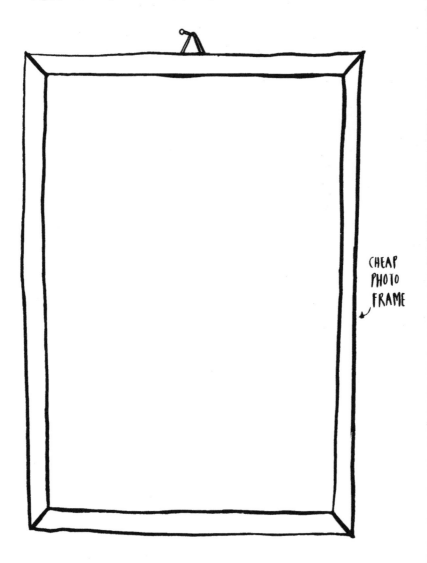

CHEAP PHOTO FRAME

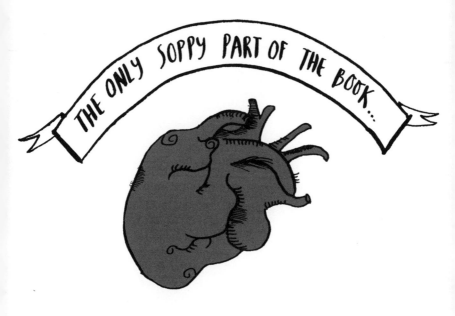

THE ONLY SOPPY PART OF THE BOOK...

BY THIS POINT OF THE BOOK, YOU MAY
HAVE FOUND SOMEONE, LEFT SOMEONE,
OR GOT A RESTRAINING ORDER FROM
SOMEONE. AS LONG AS YOU FEEL
BETTER, THAT'S WHAT COUNTS. EVEN
IF YOU ARE STILL SINGLE, THINK OF
HOW MUCH YOU HAVE COME THROUGH.
YOU'VE DONE ME PROUD. NOW, GIVE
YOURSELF A PAT ON THE BACK. NO
REALLY, DO IT.

WRITE A LETTER TO YOUR FUTURE SELF. SEAL IT IN
AN ENVELOPE WITH SOME MONEY. RE-OPEN IN FIVE
YEARS TO REALIZE HOW FAR YOU HAVE COME. THEN
BE OVERJOYED BY THE FACT YOU HAVE MONEY YOU
FORGOT ABOUT. HELL YEAH!

HELLO FUTURE ME. I HAVE OVERCOME
A LOT RECENTLY AND NOW FEEL AMAZING.
THIS IS BECAUSE...

GOOD
THINGS
COME TO THOSE
WHO
WAIT

WRITE YOUR OWN HAPPY ENDING

THEN DRAW SOME FAIRY-TALE STUFF AROUND IT.

A TRUE LOVE'S KISS HAD AWOKEN
ME FROM...

The END...

DESIGN YOUR OWN BOOK COVER:

ARE YOU IN AN EROTIC EMBRACE? OR MAYBE YOU'RE ON YOUR OWN, LOOKING TOUGH? GO ON, GIVE MOANING VAMPIRES AND BOY WIZARDS A RUN FOR THEIR MONEY.

I AM FIERCE

♪♪ ♪♪ PLAYLIST ♪♪ ♪

YOU'VE GOT A NEWFOUND CONFIDENCE AND EVERYTHING
IS GOING REALLY WELL FOR YOU. MAKE A PLAYLIST TO
PUT ON YOUR IPOD FOR THAT EXTRA BIT OF "DON'T GET
IN MY WAY OR I WILL TAKE YOU DOWN" FEELING YOU
LOVE TO HAVE IN THE MORNING.

DESIGN YOUR OWN CD COVER

♪♪♪ TRACKLIST ♪♪

1
2
3
4
5
6
7
8
9
10

DRAW ALL THE THINGS YOU HAVE
OVERCOME RECENTLY, THEN SCRIBBLE
MOTIVATIONAL QUOTES ALL OVER THEM.

CRAP THINGS I OVERCAME:

COLOR ME IN

LOVE

ADVENTURE

BEING

IS AN IN HUMAN

THE GOLDEN APPLE

IMAGINE YOU'RE A GOLDEN APPLE AT THE TOP OF A TREE.

EVERYBODY WANTS THE GOLDEN APPLE BUT THEY CANNOT REACH IT.

THE ONLY APPLES THEY CAN REACH ARE THE MOLDY ONES THAT HAVE FALLEN.

BECAUSE THEY CAN'T REACH THE GOLDEN APPLE, THEY SETTLE FOR THE BAD ONES...

IT'S NOT UNTIL SOMEONE CLIMBS ALL THE WAY TO THE TOP OF THE TREE TO PICK YOU...

THAT IS WHO IS WORTH YOUR ATTENTION. THE END.

DRAW YOURSELF AS THE GOLDEN APPLE...

REMEMBER...

YOU'RE A GOLDEN APPLE

FIN

THANK YOU

I'M GOING TO KEEP THIS SHORT AND SWEET. THANK YOU TO THE LOVELY FOLKS AT HUCK & PUCKER, MY BUDDIES IN LONDON, BRIGHTON, AND MANCHESTER (YOU KNOW WHO YOU ARE), AND FINALLY TO MY MUM, DAD, AND SISTER FOR THEIR CONTINUED SUPPORT AND BRUTAL HONESTY. I PROMISE, ONE DAY I WILL BUY YOU AN ISLAND. IF NOT THAT, THEN MAYBE A NEW HOOVER...